A **Literature Kit**™ F O R

Dear Mr. Henshaw

● ● ● ● ● ● ● ● ● ● ● ● ● ● ● ● ● ● ●

By Beverly Cleary

Written by Marie-Helen Goyetche

GRADES 5 - 6

Classroom Complete Press
P.O. Box 19729
San Diego, CA 92159
Tel: 1-800-663-3609 / Fax: 1-800-663-3608
Email: service@classroomcompletepress.com

www.classroomcompletepress.com

ISBN-13: 978-1-55319-447-7
ISBN-10: 1-55319-447-0
© 2009

Critical Thinking Skills

Dear Mr. Henshaw

Skills For Critical Thinking	Section Questions									Writing Tasks	Graphic Organizers
	One	Two	Three	Four	Five	Six	Seven	Eight	Nine		
LEVEL 1 Remembering											
• Identify Story Elements		✓		✓		✓	✓				
• Recall Details	✓	✓	✓	✓	✓	✓	✓	✓	✓	✓	✓
• Match	✓	✓	✓	✓	✓		✓	✓			
• Sequence Events			✓			✓			✓		
LEVEL 2 Understanding											
• Compare and Contrast				✓					✓		✓
• Summarize	✓	✓	✓	✓	✓	✓	✓	✓			
• State Main Idea	✓			✓		✓					
• Describe			✓	✓		✓			✓		
• Classify											
LEVEL 3 Applying											
• Plan		✓	✓	✓		✓					
• Interview					✓					✓	
• Infer Outcomes	✓	✓	✓			✓					
LEVEL 4 Analysing											
• Draw Conclusions	✓	✓	✓	✓	✓	✓	✓	✓	✓	✓	
• Identify Supporting Evidence	✓		✓	✓							✓
• Motivations	✓	✓	✓	✓	✓	✓	✓				
• Identify Cause and Effect			✓	✓				✓			✓
LEVEL 5 Evaluating											
• State & Defend An Opinion	✓	✓	✓	✓	✓	✓	✓	✓	✓	✓	✓
• Make Judgements		✓	✓	✓	✓	✓	✓	✓		✓	✓
LEVEL 6 Creating											
• Predict	✓	✓	✓	✓	✓	✓	✓	✓	✓	✓	
• Design			✓		✓			✓		✓	
• Create			✓							✓	
• Imagine Alternatives			✓				✓		✓	✓	

Based on Bloom's Taxonomy

Contents

● ● ● ● ● ● ● ● ● ● ● ● ● ● ● ● ● ● ●

🍎 TEACHER GUIDE

✏️ STUDENT HANDOUTS

✔ **6 BONUS Activity Pages!** Additional worksheets for your students

FREE!

* Go to our website: **www.classroomcompletepress.com/bonus**
* Enter item CC2514 – Dear Mr. Henshaw
* Enter pass code CC2514D for Activity Pages

Assessment Rubric

• •

Dear Mr. Henshaw

Student's Name: _____ Assignment: _____ Level: _____

Criteria	Level 1	Level 2	Level 3	Level 4
Comprehension of Novel	Demonstrates a limited understanding of the novel	Demonstrates a basic understanding of the novel	Demonstrates a good understanding of the novel	Demonstrates a thorough understanding of the novel
Content • Information and details relevant to focus	Elements incomplete; key details missing	Some elements complete; details missing	All required elements completed; key details contain some description	All required elements completed; enough description for clarity
Style • Effective word choice and originality • Precise language	Little variety in word choice. Language vague and imprecise	Some variety in word choice. Language somewhat vague and imprecise	Good variety in word choice. Language precise and quite descriptive	Writer's voice is apparent throughout. Excellent choice of words. Precise language
Conventions • Spelling, language, capitalization, punctuation	Errors seriously interfere with the writer's purpose	Repeated errors in mechanics and usage	Some errors in convention	Few errors in convention

NEXT STEPS:

WEAKNESSES:

STRENGTHS:

Dear Mr. Henshaw CC2514

Teacher Guide

Our resource has been created for ease of use by both TEACHERS and STUDENTS alike.

Introduction

Dear Mr. Henshaw is the story about a young boy called Leigh Botts. Leigh is dealing with his parents' divorce, moving to a new town, attending a new school and having someone stealing his lunch from his lunchbag. He deals with the hardship by writing to his favorite author, who suggests he start up a diary. Leigh works on his writing skills by writing regularly and it helps him to work out his issues too.

How Is Our Literature Kit™ Organized?

STUDENT HANDOUTS

Chapter Activities (*in the form of reproducible worksheets*) make up the majority of this resource. For each chapter or group of chapters there are BEFORE YOU READ activities and AFTER YOU READ activities.

- The BEFORE YOU READ activities prepare students for reading by setting a purpose for reading. They stimulate background knowledge and experience, and guide students to make connections between what they know and what they will learn. Important concepts and vocabulary from the chapter(s) are also presented.

- The AFTER YOU READ activities check students' comprehension and extend their learning. Students are asked to give thoughtful consideration of the text through creative and evaluative short-answer questions and journal prompts.

Six **Writing Tasks** and three **Graphic Organizers** are included to further develop students' critical thinking and writing skills, and analysis of the text. (*See page 6 for suggestions on using the Graphic Organizers.*) The **Assessment Rubric** (*page 4*) is a useful tool for evaluating students' responses to the Writing Tasks and Graphic Organizers.

PICTURE CUES

This resource contains three main types of pages, each with a different purpose and use. A **Picture Cue** at the top of each page shows, at a glance, what the page is for.

Teacher Guide
- Information and tools for the teacher

Student Handout
- Reproducible worksheets and activities

Easy Marking™ Answer Key
- Answers for student activities

EASY MARKING™ ANSWER KEY

Marking students' worksheets is fast and easy with this **Answer Key**. Answers are listed in columns – just line up the column with its corresponding worksheet, as shown, and see how every question matches up with its answer!

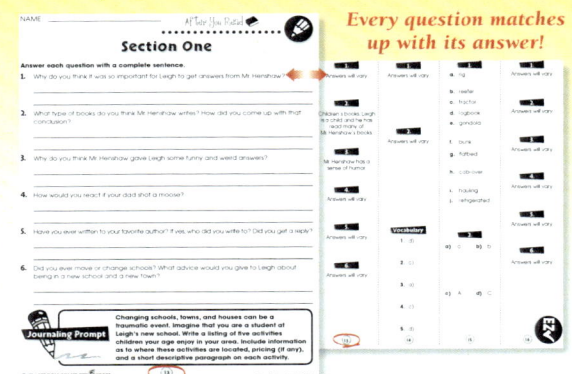

Every question matches up with its answer!

1,2,3
Graphic Organizers

The three **Graphic Organizers** included in this **Literature Kit™** are especially suited to a study of **Dear Mr. Henshaw**. Below are suggestions for using each organizer in your classroom. They may also be adapted to suit the individual needs of your students. The organizers can be used on a projection system or interactive whiteboard in teacher-led activities, and/or photocopied for use as student worksheets. To evaluate students' responses to any of the organizers, you may wish to use the **Assessment Rubric** (on page 4).

LETTER WRITING

Have a discussion with your students on the importance of a standard friendly letter. There is certain specific information which should be included in the letter, such as the return address and the date (month, day and year), both in the upper right-hand corner, the salutation (indicating who is the letter's recipient) in the upper left-hand corner, and a division of the letter into no less than 3 paragraphs. The ending of the letter should include closing remarks, and then the writer's signature. The last box to fill in is the P.S. (postscript), also known as an afterthought.

Found on Page 53.

LEIGH'S JOURNEY

In this graphic organizer, the students can refer to the map and locate where Mr. Henshaw is writing from, and where everyone lives or has lived. Most importantly, they can visualize Leigh's dad's journey. Have students calculate the miles from one place to another. This activity can also be a good tool for improving map reading skills.

Found on Page 54.

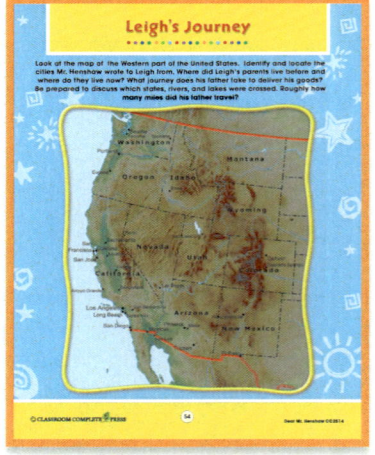

LEIGH'S EMOTIONS REPORT

Leigh will encounter many emotions during the story. In the first column of bubbles, have the student identify the emotion. In the second column, have the students analyze how Leigh dealt with this emotion. In the third column, ask how they would react to this emotion. At the end, have the students compare themselves to Leigh. Are they similar? Different? Are they compatible or not?

Found on Page 55.

Bloom's Taxonomy* for Reading Comprehension

The activities in this resource engage and build the full range of thinking skills that are essential for students' reading comprehension. Based on the six levels of thinking in Bloom's Taxonomy, questions are given that challenge students to not only recall what they have read, but to move beyond this to understand the text through higher-order thinking. By using higher-order skills of applying, analysing, evaluating and creating, students become active readers, drawing more meaning from the text, and applying and extending their learning in more sophisticated ways.

This **Literature Kit**™, therefore, is an effective tool for any Language Arts program. Whether it is used in whole or in part, or adapted to meet individual student needs, this resource provides teachers with the important questions to ask, inspiring students' interest and creativity, and promoting meaningful learning.

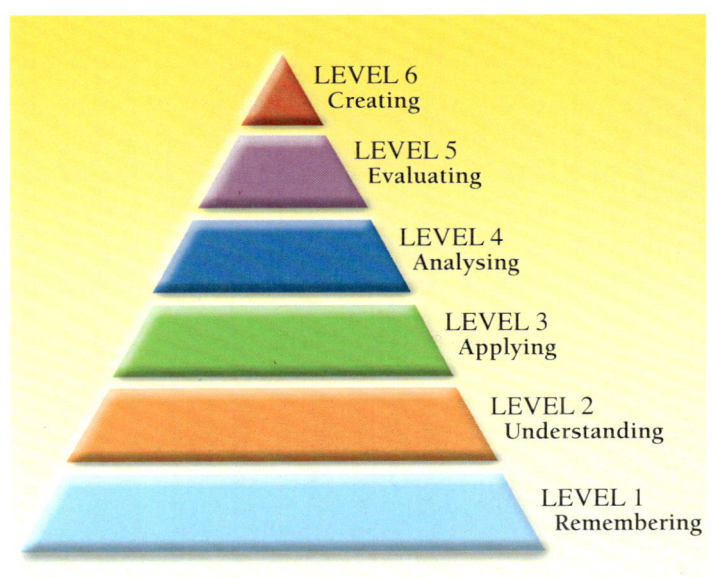

BLOOM'S TAXONOMY: 6 LEVELS OF THINKING

Bloom's Taxonomy is a tool widely used by educators for classifying learning objectives, and is based on the work of Benjamin Bloom.

Teaching Strategies   INDEPENDENT, SMALL GROUP OR WHOLE CLASS STUDY

Dear Mr. Henshaw is a novel that may be approached in several ways. Most obvious is as a traditional, whole-class read-aloud in which the teacher reads the book out loud to the entire class, stopping after one or more chapters for the students to answer the chapter questions. As they complete the questions, students reread the chapter(s) on their own. Depending on the interests and needs of your students, you may choose to apply some shared or modeled reading, focusing discussion on the author's skills, choices made in writing, and the elements of the narrative. The BEFORE YOU READ and AFTER YOU READ activities in our **Literature Kit**™ provide a basis for such discussions.

To facilitate small group and independent study learning, these activities have been divided into chapter groupings to allow students to work on manageable sections of the novel, and not feel overwhelmed by the activities. Teachers may also choose to use only a selection of the activities in this resource for small group or independent study, assigning tasks that match students' specific needs, and allowing students to work at their own speed. The components of this resource make it flexible and easy to adapt as not all of the activities need to be completed.

Teachers may wish to have their students keep a daily reading log so that they might record their daily progress and reflections. Journaling prompts have been included at the end of each chapter section to facilitate students' thinking and writing.

Summary of the Story

Leigh Botts is a typical grade 6 boy who's dealing with many issues. He's dealing with his parents' divorce, his mom has to work and goes to school while his dad drives a rig and is always on the road. Because of his parents' divorce, Leigh has to move and to change schools. He doesn't have any friends and to make things even worse, someone is stealing items from his lunchbag daily. One good thing Leigh has is a love for reading and writing. Leigh writes to Boyd Henshaw, his favorite author, on a regular basis, helping him to develop good writing skills, but also giving him a chance to reflect on the changes around him and to deal with his loneliness.

Suggestions for Further Reading

OTHER BOOKS BY BEVERLY CLEARY

Henry Huggins (illus. by Louis Darling) © 1950

Ellen Tebbits (illus. by Louis Darling) © 1951

Henry and Beezus (illus. by Louis Darling) © 1952

Otis Spofford (illus. by Louis Darling) © 1953

Henry and Ribsy (illus. by Louis Darling) © 1954

Beezus and Ramona (illus. by Louis Darling) © 1955

Fifteen (illus. by Joe and Beth Krush) © 1956

Henry and the Paper Route (illus. by Louis Darling) © 1957

Jean and Johnny (illus. by Joe and Beth Krush) © 1959

Henry and the Clubhouse (illus. by Louis Darling) © 1962

Sister of the Bride (illus. by Joe and Beth Krush) © 1963

Ribsy (illus. by Louis Darling) © 1964

The Mouse and the Motorcycle (illus. by Louis Darling) © 1965

Mitch and Amy (illus. by Bob Marstall) © 1967

Ramona the Pest (illus. by Louis Darling) © 1968

Runaway Ralph (illus. by Louis Darling) © 1970

Socks (illus. by Beatrice Darwin) © 1973

Ramona the Brave (illus. by Alan Tiegreen) © 1975

Ramona and Her Father (illus. by Alan Tiegreen) © 1977   *Ramona and Her Mother* (illus. by Alan Tiegreen) © 1979

Ramona Quimby, Age 8 (illus. by Alan Tiegreen) © 1981   *Ralph S. Mouse* (illus. by Paul O. Zelinsky) © 1982

Dear Mr. Henshaw (illus. by Paul O. Zelinsky) © 1983   *Ramona Forever* (illus. by Alan Tiegreen) © 1984

Lucky Chuck (illus. by J. Winslow Higginbottom) © 1984   *A Girl from Yamhill: A Memoir* © 1988

Muggie Maggie (illus. by Kay Life) © 1990   *Strider* (illus. by Paul O. Zelinsky) © 1991

Petey's Bedtime Story (illus. by David Small) © 1993   *My Own Two Feet* © 1995

The Hullabaloo ABC (illus. by Ted Rand) © 1998   *Ramona's World* (illus. by Alan Tiegreen) © 1999

List of Vocabulary

SECTION ONE
• amuse • argument • bulletin • duplicated • enclosure • howled • mincemeat • printed • sincerely • urgent

SECTION TWO
• bandanna • college • custodian • gifted • plain • postage • potluck • refinery • talented • to-be-continued

SECTION THREE
• catering • fictitious • foil • grateful • halyard • lonesome • nuisance • partition • snitch • support

SECTION FOUR
• broiled • checkup • drooled • gooey • grain elevator • juke box • load • pseud • retainer • tourist

SECTION FIVE
• alfalfa • citizens' band • civilization • comfortable • hawks • laundromat • mimeographed • scowling • ulcers • wrath

SECTION SIX
• eucalyptus • grove • handy • molest • monarch • mossy • quivering • typewriter • uniform • weird

SECTION SEVEN
• avoid • batteries • demonstration • experimenting • license • prose • prowls • racket • snoop • thrift

SECTION EIGHT
• chattering • forefingers • honorable • judges • mention • original • plaid • plump • rejected • salad bar

SECTION NINE
• broccoli • duplex • grinned • hauls • hesitated • sailboats • shabby • towed • weigh scale • winery

Beverly Cleary

Beverly Cleary is an author you are likely to hear and read a lot about.

She was born Beverly Bunn on April 12, 1916 in McMinnville, located in Yamhill County, Oregon. Even though she lived in a small town that didn't have a library, and had trouble reading, she still came to love reading as a young child.

Her family later moved to Portland, where she attended elementary and high school. She then moved to California to get her college degree as a librarian.

In 1940, she married Clarence Cleary. Her first book Henry Huggins was published in 1950.

In 1955, she gave birth to twins – a girl and a boy, named Marrienne Elizabeth and Malcolm James. Her twins were ten years old when Beverly wrote the story of Ralph in The Mouse and the Motorcycle and they were twenty-six years old when she wrote the story of Ramona Quimby, Age 8.

Beverly has written over 30 books, now published in over twenty countries and in fifteen different languages. In 1984, she received the Newbery award for her book Dear Mr. Henshaw. Some of her famous characters are Henry Huggins, Ralph Mouse, Ramona Quimby and Leigh Botts.

If you enjoy Leigh Botts in Dear Mr. Henshaw, you will also enjoy him in the book Strider, where his adventure continues. Clarence died in 2004 and Beverly now lives in Carmel, California.

 **Did You Know?**

- **Beverly Cleary is an only child.**
- **Beverly Cleary has also written books for adult readers.**
- **Beverly Cleary's latest book, Ramona's World was published in 1999.**

Section One

1. Beverly Cleary wrote <u>Dear Mr. Henshaw</u>. Are you familiar with her books? If yes, which books have you read?

_____

_____

_____

2. Who do you think Mr. Henshaw is? Why is he receiving a letter? Who do you think is writing to him? Why do you think letters are being written?

_____

_____

_____

Vocabulary

With a straight line, connect each word on the left with its meaning on the right.

1	**amuse**	to make copies of	a)
2	**enclosure**	to include within	b)
3	**duplicated**	already prewritten	c)
4	**sincerely**	to entertain	d)
5	**printed**	must be dealt with immediately	e)
6	**urgent**	marked by genuineness	f)

Section One

1. **Put a check mark (✓) next to the answer that is most correct.**

a) **Mr. Henshaw is well known...**
- ○ **A** as a teacher.
- ○ **B** as an author.
- ○ **C** as a truck driver.

b) **Leigh Botts is now in grade...**
- ○ **A** four.
- ○ **B** five.
- ○ **C** six.

c) **Leigh's dog's name is...**
- ○ **A** Bandit.
- ○ **B** Max.
- ○ **C** Chester.

d) **Leigh's teacher's name is...**
- ○ **A** Miss Martin.
- ○ **B** Mrs. Martinez.
- ○ **C** Miss Martinez.

e) **Leigh has asked Mr. Henshaw for...**
- ○ **A** homework tips.
- ○ **B** writing tips.
- ○ **C** cooking tips.

2. **Circle** **T** **if the statement is TRUE or** **F** **if it is FALSE.**

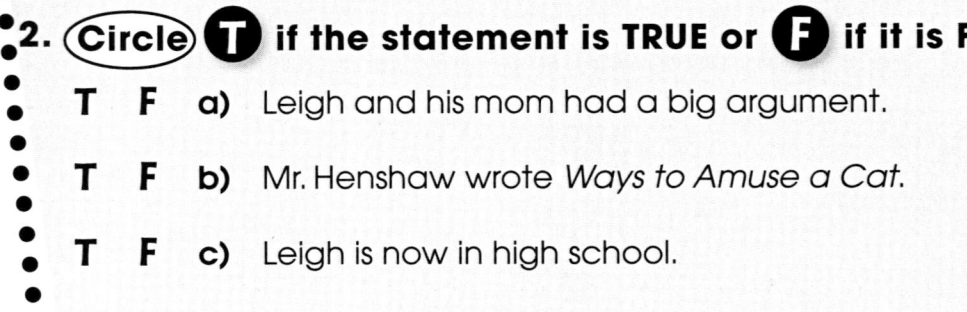

T F **a)** Leigh and his mom had a big argument.

T F **b)** Mr. Henshaw wrote *Ways to Amuse a Cat*.

T F **c)** Leigh is now in high school.

T F **d)** Mr. Henshaw wrote *Goats on Toast*.

T F **e)** Leigh sent a letter to Mr. Henshaw asking 10 questions.

Section One

Answer each question with a complete sentence.

1. Why do you think it was so important for Leigh to get answers from Mr. Henshaw?

_____

_____

2. What type of books do you think Mr. Henshaw writes? How did you come up with that conclusion?

_____

_____

3. Why do you think Mr. Henshaw gave Leigh some funny and weird answers?

_____

_____

4. How would you react if your dad shot a moose?

_____

_____

5. Have you ever written to your favorite author? If yes, who did you write to? Did you get a reply?

_____

_____

6. Did you ever move or change schools? What advice would you give to Leigh about being in a new school and a new town?

_____

_____

Journaling Prompt

Changing schools, towns, and houses can be a traumatic event. Imagine that you are a student at Leigh's new school. Write a listing of five activities children your age enjoy in your area. Include information as to where these activities are located, pricing (if any), and a short descriptive paragraph on each activity.

Section Two

1. How long do you think Leigh and Mr. Henshaw will write to each other? Do you think Leigh can make it as a writer? Why or why not?

_____

_____

_____

2. Do you think Leigh will answer Mr. Henshaw's questions? Why or why not? Why do you think Mr. Henshaw sent Leigh ten questions back?

_____

_____

_____

_____

Vocabulary

Circle the word that is <u>not</u> a synonym of the underlined word in each the following sentences.

1. Leigh considers himself to be <u>plain</u>.

a) dry   b) homely   c) fancy   d) simple

2. When placed by height, Leigh is in the <u>middle</u>.

a) average   b) moderate   c) intermediate   d) first

3. Leigh signed one of the letters *Pooped* writer.

a) rested   b) tired   c) drained   d) exhausted

4. At the end of the letter, Leigh wrote to be *continued*.

a) proceed   b) go forward   c) done   d) carry on

5. Leigh's parents are <u>divorced</u>.

a) separated   b) broke up   c) split up   d) together

Section Two

1. Use the words in the box to answer each question.

bunk	cab-over	flatbed	gondola	hauling
logbook	reefer	refrigerated	rig	tractor

[   ] **a)** What's the vehicle called where the driver sits, drives and where the motor is?

[   ] **b)** What is the name of a refrigerated trailer?

[   ] **c)** What do truckers call a truck?

[   ] **d)** Where do truckers enter in their mileage and hours?

[   ] **e)** What is the name of the container used to transport loose material?

[   ] **f)** Where does the trucker sleep?

[   ] **g)** What do you call a truck that is used to carry mobile homes?

[   ] **h)** What is the truck called when the cab is located above the engine?

[   ] **i)** What is another word for carrying or transporting?

[   ] **j)** What type of van must meat be transported in?

2. Put a check mark (✓) next to the word which best describes how each character felt about each thing / event.

a) Leigh about the cattle along Interstate 5?
- ○ **A** anxious
- ○ **B** overwhelmed
- ○ **C** bored

b) Mr. Fridley about someone throwing up in school?
- ○ **A** happy
- ○ **B** undisturbed
- ○ **C** impatient

c) Leigh about his mom leaving early for school?
- ○ **A** lonely
- ○ **B** worried
- ○ **C** annoyed

d) Bandit about riding with Dad?
- ○ **A** hyper
- ○ **B** lonesome
- ○ **C** happy

After You Read

Section Two

Answer each question with a complete sentence.

1. How would you have dealt with someone stealing your lunch?

_____

_____

2. What would motivate someone to steal someone else's lunch?

_____

_____

3. Have you ever seen something so boring like Interstate 5? What was it? Where was it?

_____

_____

4. What steps could Leigh take to make sure no one can go into his lunchbag?

_____

_____

5. Why do you think Dad can't tell Leigh that he misses him?

_____

_____

6. If you were one of the teachers at the school, what would you do about the stealing of lunch items from Leigh?

_____

_____

Journaling Prompt

Leigh's mom thinks television rots your brain. Do you agree with her? In a paragraph or two, write what your thoughts are about television. Share your views with a partner. Hold a class debate on the subject: is television good for your brain (mind) or not?

NAME: _____

Section Two

Answer each question as if Mr. Henshaw had sent them to you.

1. Who are you?

_____

_____

2. What do you look like?

_____

_____

3. What is your family like?

_____

_____

4. Where do you live?

_____

_____

5. Do you have any pets?

_____

_____

6. Do you like school?

_____

_____

7. Who are your friends?

_____

_____

8. Who is your favorite teacher?

_____

_____

9. What bothers you?

_____

_____

10. What do you wish?

_____

_____

NAME: _____

Section Three

1. Have you ever used a diary? How long did you write in it? Did anyone else read it?

_____

_____

_____

2. How do you feel about the fact that Leigh feels lonely? What would you suggest he do to get out of the loneliness phase?

_____

_____

_____

Vocabulary

Replace the words in brackets in the sentences below with a word from the word list.

fictitious	foil	halyard	partition	pretend	snitch

1. The kid in the store was playing (make believe) _____ when he was there with his mom.

2. Leigh wanted to (fool) _____ the thief by writing a (made-up) _____ name.

3. He didn't want to have to (complain to the teacher) _____ about someone stealing his lunch.

4. Leigh kept an eye out all morning checking who went behind the (divider) _____.

5. Leigh was very proud to raise the U.S. flag on the (rope) _____.

Section Three

1. Put a check mark (✓) next to the answer that is most correct.

a) Mr. Fridley asked Leigh to help him with which chore?

○ **A**   Putting the garbage on the side of the road.
○ **B**   Raising the flag in the morning.
○ **C**   Making canapés for lunchtime.

b) Leigh found one way to stop the thief from stealing his lunch. How?

○ **A**   He kept his lunch with him at all times.
○ **B**   He bought his lunch at the cafeteria.
○ **C**   He ate it on his way to school.

c) What is Leigh's middle name?

○ **A**   It was Bill.
○ **B**   It was Marcus.
○ **C**   It was William.

d) What does Leigh ask Mr. Henshaw?

○ **A**   He wants to move in with him.
○ **B**   He wants Mr. Henshaw to speak at his school.
○ **C**   He wants to exchange letters and become pen pals with him.

2. Number the events from 1 to 5 in the order that they occurred.

a) Leigh, his mom and a few other people ate at Katy's for Christmas dinner.

b) Dad sent Leigh a new quilted down jacket.

c) Mom, Dad and Leigh wrote songs about the lonely shoe lying on the highway.

d) Leigh wants to write a book called "The Great Lunchbag Mystery".

e) Mr. Henshaw sent a postcard to Leigh from Wyoming.

NAME: _____

Answer each question with a complete sentence.

1. What is your opinion of Leigh?

   _____

   _____

2. What would be the consequence in your school if someone was stealing lunches?

   _____

   _____

3. What other ways could Leigh's father have shown that he cared about his son?

   _____

   _____

4. Describe the relationship between Leigh's mom and dad.

   _____

   _____

5. Many children lost their retainers when they accidentally threw them in the garbage at lunchtime. List other items people might accidentally lose at the end of lunchtime.

   _____

   _____

Journaling Prompt

Leigh talks about how the U.S. flag and the California state flag are raised every morning at his school. Do a mini-research project and find the flag of your state.

On another sheet of paper draw the state flag and your country's flag. Find out what the flags represent and what the colors, symbols and objects on them mean and represent.

NAME: _____

Section Three
The Lonely Shoe Lying on the Highway

Using your imagination, create your own story about the lonely shoe lying on the highway. You can write about how it got there, what has happened to it since and, if you like, about how it may feel (if it has feelings) about being away from the other shoe in the now separated pair.

_____
_____
_____
_____
_____
_____
_____
_____
_____
_____
_____
_____
_____
_____
_____
_____

Section Four

1. Do you think Leigh will succeed in catching the lunch thief? How do you think he will go about it?

_____

_____

2. Should Leigh's Mom get the TV fixed? Why or why not? How long could you live without the TV? The computer? Video games? The phone? Order these items' importance to your life in priority from greatest to least, noting which item(s) you could NOT do without and which you could manage to live without.

_____

_____

_____

Vocabulary

Leigh uses a lot of expressions in the story. Write, in your own words what the expressions mean.

1. Leigh's dad said *he'd* see if traveling together was a possibility.

_____

2. Leigh's dad told Leigh to *keep his nose clean*.

_____

3. Mr. Fridley told Leigh that *he might trip over his lower lip*.

_____

4. Leigh's mom wants his brain *to stay in good shape*.

_____

Section Four

1. Use the words in the box to answer each question.

| Dad | Leigh's teacher | Librarian | Mom | Mr. Fridley |

a) Who told Leigh she had something for him?

b) Who told Leigh that the call would come in the next week?

c) Who told Leigh that his writing was improving?

d) Who told Leigh that it takes two people to get a divorce?

e) Who told Leigh to cheer up?

2. Circle T if the statement is TRUE or F if it is FALSE.

T F **a)** Leigh taped up his lunch so well he had trouble getting into it.

T F **b)** Leigh's friends got together and built him a burglar alarm to protect his lunch.

T F **c)** Leigh is having a lot of difficulty with his writing skills.

T F **d)** Mr. Henshaw sent a postcard to Leigh from Kansas.

3. Choose the correct answer.

a) Dad phoned Leigh from which town?
- **A** Taft, California.
- **B** Hermiston, Oregon.
- **C** Pacific Grove, California.

b) What was bothering Leigh?
- **A** It was bothering him that he had to run to school.
- **B** It was bothering him that his dog is so demanding.
- **C** He was bothered that his lunch was getting too much attention.

c) What was Spreckels?
- **A** Leigh's favorite oatmeal.
- **B** The sugar refinery.
- **C** A fishing harbor.

NAME: _____

Section Four

Answer each question with a complete sentence.

1. How do you normally spend your Christmas holidays? What traditions are always kept year after year?

_____

_____

2. Do you think it was good idea for Leigh's teacher to tell him about the chance to win lunch with a Famous Author? Why or why not?

_____

_____

3. If you were the winner of the Famous Author contest, who would you like to have lunch with?

_____

_____

4. What is the relationship between Charlie and Mom?

_____

_____

5. If you were Leigh's parents, what would you have done to make the divorce a little easier on Leigh?

_____

_____

ASSETS	LIABILITIES

Journaling Prompt

"Three sudden brothers or sisters was something to think about," thought Leigh. **How would you feel if tomorrow morning you suddenly got three new siblings? Would you consider them assets to your family? Would they be liabilities? Recopy the T-Chart above onto another sheet of paper and see what getting three new siblings would mean to you.**

 Before You Read

Section Five

1. What type of story do you think Leigh will write? What type of story would you write?

_____

_____

_____

2. Do you think the lunch thief will strike again? How?

_____

_____

_____

Vocabulary

With a straight line, connect each word on the left with its meaning on the right.

1	**scowling**		an open sore caused by stress	**a**
2	**wrath**		bird of prey	**b**
3	**civilization**		strong vengeful anger	**c**
4	**ulcers**		a face made to show displeasure	**d**
5	**hawk**		a place to wash and dry clothes	**e**
6	**Laundromat**		a high level of cultural and technological development within a society	**f**

NAME: _____

Section Five

1. Put a check mark (✓) next to the answer that is most correct.

a) What did Leigh's dad really love?

- ○ **A** The excitement of his job.
- ○ **B** The truck stop food.
- ○ **C** The comfort of the bunk in his truck.

b) What type of friends did mom have over?

- ○ **A** Her trucker friends.
- ○ **B** Her women friends and their babies.
- ○ **C** Her sisters and other relatives.

c) When did Leigh's dad finally call?

- ○ **A** Before getting pizza with his new girlfriend and her son.
- ○ **B** Right after church before lunchtime.
- ○ **C** Leigh couldn't wait anymore so he called his dad himself.

d) In the snowstorm, what did dad lose?

- ○ **A** He lost his chains.
- ○ **B** He lost Bandit.
- ○ **C** He lost Bandit's bandanna.

2. Read the statements below. Do you AGREE or DISAGREE with each? Circle your choice and write a one sentence statement explaining why you feel the way you do in the space provided.

Agree   Disagree   **a)** Parents' lives must change when they have children.

_____

Agree   Disagree   **b)** If you tell your child that you will call you'd better call.

_____

Agree   Disagree   **c)** You can't be a trucker without a Citizens' Band radio.

_____

Agree   Disagree   **d)** Truckers must respect weight and speed limits.

NAME: _____

Section Five

Answer each question with a complete sentence.

1. If you were given the tasks of fixing a meal, babysitting some babies and doing your homework, which would you do first? Second? Third? Why would you do the chores in that order? Explain your answer.

_____

_____

2. What are other ways Leigh could have contacted his dad?

_____

_____

3. Do you believe Leigh's father, who said he was going to call him in the evening? Why or why not?

_____

_____

4. Do you think adding the words *Dear Mr. Pretend Henshaw* at the top of the letter would be helpful to you when writing in your diary? Why or why not?

_____

_____

Journaling Prompt

Leigh is getting more and more comfortable writing in his diary. His relationship with Mr. Henshaw is also growing more established as letters and postcards exchange hands between them regularly. Pretending that you are Leigh, write a new set of questions to Mr. Henshaw. Don't include any of the questions you asked during the first stages of the relationship.

Now write ten new questions from Mr. Henshaw to Leigh. Again don't include questions he would ask Leigh at the beginning of their relationship.

Compare your questions with a partner. Are the questions heading in the same direction? What are the differences?

Section Six

1. Based on relationships you have with your friends, where do you predict the relationship between Leigh and Mr. Henshaw will go from here?

_____

_____

_____

2. Do you think Leigh's parents will have a change of heart toward each other and that they will get back together again?

_____

_____

_____

Vocabulary

Somehow all the compound words in this section separated. Using a word from the box on the left along with a word from the box on the right, form the 12 possible compound words below. Some words can be used twice.

	any	bath	butter		bag	book	cake
cheese	class	lunch	mouse	card	fly	off	room
post	rip	year		time	trap	way	

1. _____ 7. _____

2. _____ 8. _____

3. _____ 9. _____

4. _____ 10. _____

5. _____ 11. _____

6. _____ 12. _____

After You Read

Section Six

1. Use the words in the box to answer each question.

lunchbag	twenty dollar bill	typewriter
batteries and a bell	butterflies	deviled crab

a) What did Leigh find floating through the trees?

b) What did Leigh put on the floor in the hallway?

c) What did Leigh's mom put in the puff shells?

d) What did Leigh's dad put in the napkin?

e) What was in the Alarm System box?

f) What did Leigh decide to save his money toward?

2. Number the events from ❶ to ❼ in the order they occurred in these sections.

a) Leigh got a postcard from his dad.

b) The cheesecake went missing, again.

c) Leigh bought one of Mr. Henshaw's books at a garage sale.

d) Leigh wrote to Mr. Henshaw and asked for advice.

e) Mr. Fridley told Leigh to 'think positively'.

f) Leigh needed to take a walk.

g) Leigh worked hard on his story about a ten-foot wax man.

Section Six

Answer each question with a complete sentence.

1. If you were Leigh, what would cheer you up?

_____

_____

2. How should Leigh go about *'thinking positively'*?

_____

_____

3. If you were Mr. Henshaw, how would you react if a fan told you they bought your book at a garage sale?

_____

_____

4. If Leigh had kicked that lunch box at your school, what would have been the consequences?

_____

_____

5. Can you relate to how Leigh was feeling? How did you cheer up?

_____

_____

6. Is it beneficial to get someone to read through a story you're writing while you are still in the process of writing it? How could they help you? Could it hurt your story? How?

_____

_____

Journaling Prompt

Leigh was upset, lonely and angry. Write a letter to Leigh and give him advice on how to deal with his feelings. Remember that your letter should contain at least 3 paragraphs. You are not writing a shopping list. Giving advice is a serious matter.

Section Six
The Monarch Butterfly

Leigh went for a walk because he felt rotten. He came to a sign that said BUTTERFLY TREES. He went into the grove, finding the butterflies so beautiful that he suddenly felt good all over.

1. What do you know about Monarch butterflies?

_____

_____

_____

_____

2. Using your school library or the internet, read up on them and discover their world, answering the following questions.

a) Where do they come from?

_____

_____

b) Why are they so special?

_____

_____

c) Where do they migrate to and from?

_____

_____

d) What predators do they have?

_____

_____

e) How do they reproduce?

_____

_____

f) What do they eat?

_____

_____

g) How do you feel when you see a Monarch butterfly?

_____

_____

NAME: _____

Section Seven

1. Leigh is realizing that his story may not be on the right track. What should he do from here?

_____

_____

_____

2. Pretend that Leigh is writing a thank-you note to his dad. What do you think he should write in it? Be creative and help him write it so that his dad will be inspired to send money again.

_____

_____

_____

Vocabulary

Replace the words in brackets in the sentences below with a word from the word list.

avoid	demonstrate	experimenting	prose	racket	thrift

1. Mom decorated the tiny house with items from the (secondhand) _____ shop.

2. Barry's sisters and stepsisters made a (lots of noise) _____.

3. Leigh kept switching from poetry to (ordinary) _____ writing.

4. Dad is a good driver but he only speeds up when he wants to (abstain) _____ getting a ticket.

5. Many teachers were impressed with Leigh's burglar alarm. He had to (show) _____ how it worked.

6. Barry and Leigh did some (investigating) _____ with the batteries and bells.

Section Seven

1. Put a check mark (✓) next to the answer that is NOT correct.

a) Leigh bought a black lunchbox.

○ **A** He got it from the thrift shop.
○ **B** He used it to carry his lunch.
○ **C** The kids made fun of him.

b) Leigh set off his alarm when he wanted to eat his lunch.

○ **A** He had to show the principal, teachers and fellow students how it worked.
○ **B** The thief was caught the next day.
○ **C** He found that other children also had things stolen from their lunch.

c) Leigh's dad called.

○ **A** He wanted to tell Leigh that he was marrying the pizza boy's mom.
○ **B** He asked Leigh if he missed *his old dad*.
○ **C** He wanted to talk to his mom so that he could tell her that the support payment would come in the following week.

d) Barry and Leigh built an alarm for Barry's room.

○ **A** Barry's sisters thought it was fun to open the door, set it off and go run and hide.
○ **B** It was driving Barry's mother crazy.
○ **C** Barry let the batteries die.

2. Circle T if the statement is TRUE or F if it is FALSE.

T F **a)** Leigh's mom is a big snoop.

T F **b)** Barry wished he could have a room that nobody ever went into.

T F **c)** Leigh's mom told Leigh that his father wasn't a bad man.

T F **d)** Leigh wanted to know if his mom could remarry again.

T F **e)** Leigh went back to visit the Monarch butterflies.

NAME: _____

Section Seven

Answer each question with a complete sentence.

1. What do you think about Leigh's mother working and going to school?

_____

_____

2. Why do you think Leigh's mother didn't want to talk to his dad?

_____

_____

3. Why would the little girls get a kick out of getting the alarm to ring?

_____

_____

4. Could you build your own alarm (door or lunch alarm)? Where would you get the information on how to do it?

_____

_____

5. What can you conclude about Leigh by the way he thinks of the person who stole his lunch?

_____

_____

6. What do you think will happen to the lunch thief from now on?

_____

_____

Journaling Prompt

Tomorrow is the big day. The Young Writers' Yearbook will be given out. Maybe Leigh will be lucky, win and get to go have lunch with the Famous Author.

Write a new diary entry for Leigh. How does he feel? Will he be able to sleep? Is he excited? Does he really have reason to believe he has a good chance at winning?

Section Eight

1. How well do you think Leigh will do with his story for the Young Writers' Yearbook? Do you think he has a winning entry? Why or why not?

_____

_____

_____

2. Leigh and Barry are developing a friendship. Think of one of your friends. Why is he or she your friend? What is it that you appreciate about that person? What do you hope they appreciate about you?

_____

_____

_____

Vocabulary

Choose the correct word that matches the definition.

author	autograph	imitate	plagiarism	published	rejected

1. Copying someone else's work and calling it your own is called _____.

2. Having one's work printed can also be called being _____.

3. The writer of a written piece is the _____.

4. To be like or to appear to be like is to _____.

5. Publishing houses don't accept every story they read. That's why many stories have been _____.

6. A person's handwritten signature written as a souvenir is called an _____.

After You Read 📖

Section Eight

1. **Use the people in the box below to answer each question.**

Miss.Martinez	Miss.Neely	Mr.Badger	Mr.Henshaw	Mrs.Badger	the judges

[_____] **a)** Who sat with the librarians?

[_____] **b)** Who did Leigh happen to be dressed like?

[_____] **c)** Who asked Leigh if he wanted to meet the Famous Author?

[_____] **d)** Who remembered Leigh's piece?

[_____] **e)** Who made the students write to an author?

[_____] **f)** Who never agreed during writing contests?

2. **Put a check mark (✓) next to the word or phrase which best describes how the character(s) felt about each event.**

a) Leigh when he saw that he hadn't won?
- ○ **A** disappointed
- ○ **B** relieved
- ○ **C** angry

b) The kids that didn't win at all?
- ○ **A** tired
- ○ **B** mad
- ○ **C** inspired

c) The girls when they met Mrs. Angela Badger?
- ○ **A** sad
- ○ **B** shy
- ○ **C** excited

d) Leigh when he found out the author wasn't Mr. Henshaw?
- ○ **A** angry
- ○ **B** glad
- ○ **C** embarrassed

e) The librarians when they ate with Mr. Badger?
- ○ **A** talkative & amused
- ○ **B** nervous
- ○ **C** shy & quiet

f) Leigh when Mrs. Badger asked him about his piece?
- ○ **A** sick
- ○ **B** upset
- ○ **C** embarrassed

After You Read 📖

Section Eight

Answer each question with a complete sentence.

1. How do you get inspired when your teacher gives you a writing assignment to do? Do you try and try again like Leigh? Explain.

_____

_____

2. Can you recall how Leigh felt when Mrs. Badger called him an author and remembered his piece of writing?

_____

_____

3. What do think about Mrs. Badger?

_____

_____

4. If you were the winner of this contest, which author would you like to meet? Why?

_____

_____

5. Did you know there's a real author called Angela Badger? What kind of information can you find on her? Is the character in the book based on the real Angela Badger?

_____

_____

_____

_____

_____

Journaling Prompt

Go back and read the advice that Mrs. Badger gives Leigh. Create a to-do list for writing based on what she has suggested, also including the advice Mr. Henshaw has given.

Design a 'writing tips' poster which you can hang up either in the classroom, library or where you do your homework at home.

NAME: _____

Section Nine

1. Leigh was very happy to have had lunch with Mrs. Badger even if he hadn't read her books. Do you think that will inspire him to read her books? Why or why not?

_____

_____

2. The book is almost over. Do you think Leigh will meet his favorite author? Do you predict that his parents might get back together again? Will Leigh make new friends? Will the lunch thief strike again?

_____

_____

Vocabulary - Crossword

Word List

Bandanna	rig
broccoli	sailboats
bunk	tavern
grin	weighscale
grove	winery

Across

2. Bandit was wearing a red one.
4. Where Leigh and his dad hauled the grapes to.
5. Where Dad sleeps.
7. Barry and Leigh sat on a rock to watch them.
8. Where the butterflies were.
9. Dad only had a half of one.

Down

1. Where mom accused dad of being on Saturday nights.
3. Where the other trucker gave Bandit back to Dad.
5. Dad's waiting for a reefer loaded with it.
6. Dad hauls the refrigerated reefers in this.

Section Nine

1. Number the events from ❶ to ❼ in the order that they occurred.

☐ **a)** Leigh's mom made and served two cups of coffee.

☐ **b)** Leigh found that Bandit now wears a new red bandanna.

☐ **c)** Barry and Leigh watched the sailboats on the bay.

☐ **d)** Leigh's dad was going to leave Bandit with him but Leigh thought Bandit should keep his dad company on the road.

☐ **e)** Leigh's parents still think about each other but their relationship can't be worked out.

☐ **f)** Leigh's mom drove up and got out of the car.

☐ **g)** Dad and Bandit were parked in front of Leigh's house.

2. Read the statements below. Do you AGREE or DISAGREE with each? Circle your choice and write a one sentence statement explaining why you feel the way you do in the space provided.

Agree   Disagree   a) The dog should have stayed with Leigh.

_____

Agree   Disagree   b) Parents shouldn't discuss problems or fight in front of their kids.

_____

Agree   Disagree   c) People who love each other should stay together.

_____

Agree   Disagree   d) Leigh's dad will now be a better dad to him.

_____

Agree   Disagree   e) It is important for parents to tell children they are proud of them.

_____

NAME: _____

Section Nine

Answer each question with a complete sentence.

1. Why do you think Leigh's dad really came for a visit?

_____

_____

2. Do you like the way the book ends? Explain your answer.

_____

_____

3. If you were Leigh's dad, how would you have reacted to what Leigh's mom said?

_____

_____

4. If you were Leigh's mom, how would you have reacted to what Leigh's dad said?

_____

_____

5. Would you have given the dog to your dad? Explain your answer.

_____

_____

6. What do you think about Leigh from the beginning of the book till the end?

_____

_____

Journaling Prompt

'*I felt sad and a whole lot better at the same* time,' thought Leigh.

This is how the book ends. Explain why Leigh feels sad and a whole lot better at the same time.

If you were to write a sequel to <u>Dear Mr. Henshaw</u>, where would you see these characters go? Write a synopsis for the sequel, <u>Dear Mr. Henshaw II</u>.

Sections One and Two: Letter Writing

Who is your favorite author? You might be able to find your favorite author's mailing address on the internet, or you can mail the letter right to the publishing company that published his or her book.

Using the format from the graphic organizer, write a letter to your favorite author. Explain what you admire about the author's work, offer advice or ideas, and add anything else you might like to say. Check your letter for spelling mistakes. Make sure that the questions you ask <u>aren't</u> so simple that the information they ask for can be found without asking the author (for example, don't ask the author's birthday, as you could probably find the answer to that very easily by checking in a book or on the internet).

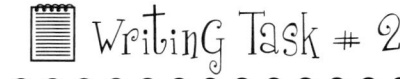 

Section Three: Asking Interesting Questions

Leigh sent Mr. Henshaw many questions. In return, Mr. Henshaw answered the questions with funny answers and sent Leigh a list of ten questions.

Your task is to write ten questions you would want to ask your favorite author. Your questions should not be answerable with a simple 'yes' or 'no'. Open - ended questions, where the person has to really think and reply in one or more sentences are the type of questions to ask. Make sure that the information isn't already found on his or her web site. Be creative.

Section Four:
Catering Company

Imagine that you are going to open your very own catering company. You will need to develop a menu, filled with canapés, quiches, deviled eggs and other finger foods people like to munch on at parties.

Find yourself a creative company name. Create a menu and write your recipes. Work out how you would make people in your area aware of your catering business. How would you handle issues such as food allergies and differing cultures' diverse food preferences?

 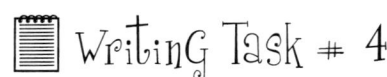 📋 Writing Task # 4

Sections Five and Six:
Postcard for Leigh

Leigh is getting many postcards. Some are from Mr. Henshaw and others are from his dad. Pretend that you are going to send Leigh a postcard.

Design an original postcard to send to Leigh based on everything that you know about him. Color it and fill in the back with a special message to Leigh.

Sections Seven and Eight: Welcome Speech

You have just won first place at this year's Young Writers Yearbook. You have been asked to write the introductory speech and to welcome Mr. Boyd Henshaw as the Famous Author guest.

Write your speech, welcoming everyone, introducing Mr. Henshaw, and discussing some of the most important accomplishments Mr. Henshaw has achieved as an author. The speech should try to make Mr. Henshaw feel special, and feel that his work is appreciated and respected by young readers.

Section Nine: Keep in Touch

In <u>Dear Mr. Henshaw,</u> there's a friendship that develops between Leigh and Mr. Henshaw. Leigh sent his first letter to Mr. Henshaw when he was in grade 2, and their relationship grew until Leigh was in grade 6, in a new town and a new school.

Imagine that their communication had stopped there. It's now twenty-five years later.

Write a letter to Leigh from Mr. Henshaw telling him about his latest accomplishments and any changes which have occurred over the past 25 years. Then have Leigh write back, telling Mr. Henshaw about the events and changes in his life. Be creative and try to be realistic in your depictions of these characters as they have matured.

NAME: _____

Word Search Puzzle

Find all of the words in the Word Search. Words are written horizontally, vertically, diagonally, and some are even written backwards.

AMUSE
AUTHOR
BANDANNA
BATTERIES
BROCCOLI
CATERING
DEMONSTRATION
DESCRIPTION
DUPLICATED
EXPERIMENTING
FOIL
LICENSE
LOAD
MONARCH
NUISANCE
POSTAGE
POSTCARD
POTLUCK
PRINTED
PROSE
REEFER
REFINERY
REJECTED
RIG
SINCERELY
TALENTED
THIEF
TYPEWRITER
URGENT
WRITER

D	E	M	O	N	S	T	R	A	T	I	O	N	E	S	U	M	A
A	B	B	R	O	C	C	O	L	I	C	D	U	E	F	G	H	U
W	R	T	M	O	S	B	H	J	Q	F	O	I	L	O	A	D	T
R	R	E	T	I	R	W	E	P	Y	T	F	S	I	N	R	O	H
I	G	T	A	L	E	N	T	E	D	X	V	A	C	E	I	Y	O
T	J	D	H	R	Y	W	Q	P	K	L	N	N	E	B	G	A	R
N	C	X	Z	I	A	R	R	W	Q	L	P	C	N	H	S	T	E
G	N	I	T	N	E	M	I	R	E	P	X	E	S	C	N	M	J
P	I	X	F	G	H	F	K	H	D	S	R	A	E	E	I	G	E
O	C	X	C	A	T	E	R	I	N	G	J	A	G	U	E	S	C
S	I	N	C	E	R	E	L	Y	L	K	J	R	B	R	V	M	T
T	H	G	F	D	S	A	W	E	T	Y	U	O	P	K	H	B	E
C	B	V	C	G	F	D	N	O	I	T	P	I	R	C	S	E	D
A	Y	B	A	T	T	E	R	I	E	S	U	O	P	K	G	F	U
R	O	A	L	N	G	U	Y	T	R	E	G	B	G	J	F	A	P
D	F	N	I	Y	R	H	N	H	C	R	A	N	O	M	F	A	L
E	I	D	O	P	R	H	B	A	S	D	F	G	H	J	K	R	I
T	T	A	A	S	P	O	S	T	A	G	E	B	F	X	E	E	C
N	E	N	R	T	P	O	T	L	U	C	K	U	T	T	D	S	A
I	D	N	Y	R	E	N	I	F	E	R	O	P	I	J	K	T	T
R	R	A	A	V	B	H	R	E	E	F	E	R	M	N	S	O	E
P	R	O	S	E	S	L	A	U	G	D	W	L	H	V	W	O	D

After You Read

Comprehension Quiz

Answer each question in a complete sentence.

1. How did Leigh feel about <u>Ways to Amuse a Dog</u>? Who wrote the book?

_____

_____

2. How did Leigh get stuck answering ten questions? What wouldn't he get if he didn't answer the questions?

_____

_____

3. Where is Leigh's dad? What does he do for a living? What does Leigh's mom do for a living?

_____

_____

4. What type of pet does Leigh have? What is its name?

_____

_____

5. What was getting Leigh super angry? Why was he so lonesome?

_____

_____

6. How was he going to solve his biggest problem at school? Who would help him?

_____

_____

7. Who does Leigh share his problems with? How did he get started?

_____

_____

SUBTOTAL: /15

Comprehension Quiz

1. (Circle) **T** if the statement is **TRUE** or **F** if it is **FALSE.**   **7**

T   F   a)   Leigh had a brother named Chuck.

T   F   b)   He loved to eat food from Catering by Katy.

T   F   c)   Leigh is now in grade 6.

T   F   d)   Leigh's favorite author is Angela Badger.

T   F   e)   Leigh wrote a story about monsters for the Famous Writers Yearbook.

T   F   f)   Leigh met Mr. Henshaw when he got to high school.

T   F   g)   Leigh told his dad to keep Bandit because he didn't have any way to amuse him.

2. Put a check mark (✓) next to the answer that is most correct.

a) What was the fictitious name Leigh wrote on his lunchbag?   **1**
- ○ **A**   Joe Baker.
- ○ **B**   Joe Fridley.
- ○ **C**   Joe Kelly.

b) What grade was Leigh in when he first wrote to Mr. Henshaw?   **1**
- ○ **A**   He was in grade one.
- ○ **B**   He was in grade two.
- ○ **C**   He was in grade three.

c) What impressed Leigh the most about Mrs. Angela Badger?   **1**
- ○ **A**   She called him Mr. Botts.
- ○ **B**   She helped him get salad at the salad bar.
- ○ **C**   She called him an author.

SUBTOTAL: /10

Bonus

What was the title of Leigh's honorable mention?
- ○ **A**   "A Day on Dad's Rig."
- ○ **B**   "A Day on Dad's Reefer."
- ○ **C**   "A Day on Dad's Tractor."

1. Answers will vary
2. Answers will vary
3. Answers will vary
4. Answers will vary
5. Answers will vary
6. Answers will vary

(16)

1.
a. rig
b. reefer
c. tractor
d. logbook
e. gondola
f. bunk
g. flatbed
h. cab-over
i. hauling
j. refrigerated

2. a) c b) b
c) A d) C

(15)

---

1. Answers will vary
2. Answers will vary

Vocabulary
1. d)
2. c)
3. a)
4. c)
5. d)

(14)

---

1. Answers will vary
2. Children's books. Leigh is a child and he has read many of Mr. Henshaw's books.
3. Mr. Henshaw has a sense of humor.
4. Answers will vary
5. Answers will vary
6. Answers will vary

(13)

1.
a) B
b) C
c) A
d) C
e) B

2.
a) T
b) F
c) F
d) F
e) T

(12)

---

1. Answers will vary
2. Answers will vary

Vocabulary
1. d)
2. b)
3. a)
4. f)
5. c)
6. e)

(11)

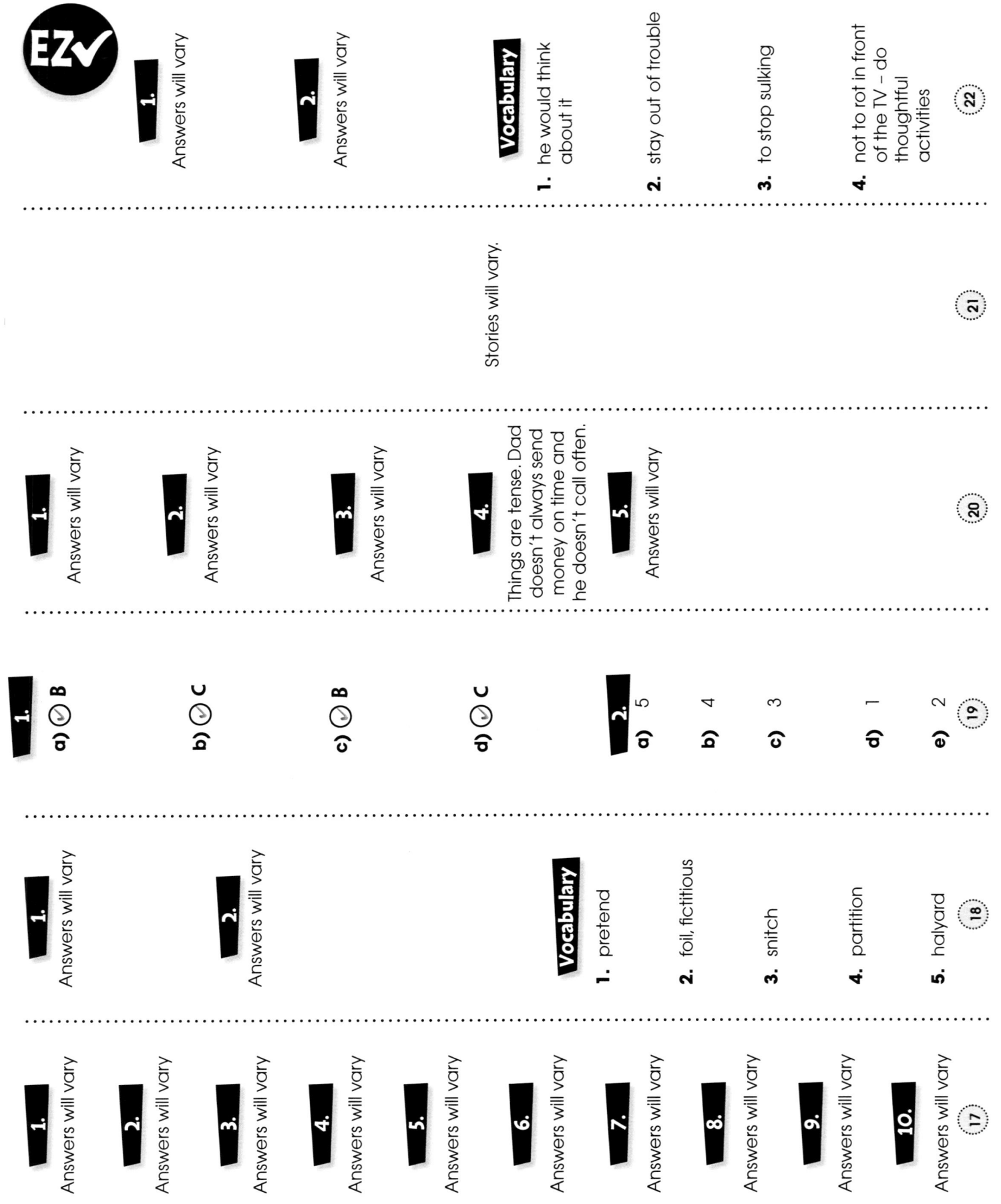

EZ✓

1. Answers will vary

2. Answers will vary

Vocabulary

1. he would think about it

2. stay out of trouble

3. to stop sulking

4. not to rot in front of the TV – do thoughtful activities

(22)

Stories will vary.

(21)

1. Answers will vary

2. Answers will vary

3. Answers will vary

4. Things are tense. Dad doesn't always send money on time and he doesn't call often.

5. Answers will vary

(20)

1.
a) ✓ B
b) ✓ C
c) ✓ B
d) ✓ C

2.
a) 5
b) 4
c) 3
d) 1
e) 2

(19)

1. Answers will vary

2. Answers will vary

Vocabulary

1. pretend

2. foil, fictitious

3. snitch

4. partition

5. halyard

(18)

1. Answers will vary
2. Answers will vary
3. Answers will vary
4. Answers will vary
5. Answers will vary
6. Answers will vary
7. Answers will vary
8. Answers will vary
9. Answers will vary
10. Answers will vary

(17)

1. Answers will vary

2. Answers will vary

(28)

---

1. Answers will vary

2. Answers will vary

3. Answers will vary

4. Answers will vary

(27)

1.
a) ✓ A

b) ✓ B

c) ✓ C

d) ✓ B

2. Answers will vary

(26)

---

1. Answers will vary

2. Answers will vary

Vocabulary
1. d
2. c
3. f
4. a
5. b
6. e

(25)

---

1. Answers will vary

2. Answers will vary

3. Answers will vary

4. They went on some dates – there is no relationship between them.

5. Answers will vary

(24)

1.
a) Librarian
b) Dad
c) Leigh's teacher
d) Mom
e) Mr. Fridley

2.
a) T
b) F
c) F
d) F

3.
a) ✓ B

b) ✓ C

c) ✓ B

(23)

EZ✓

1. Answers will vary

2. Answers will vary

3. Answers will vary

4. Answers will vary

5. Answers will vary

6. Answers will vary

(34)

1.
a) ◯ C
b) ◯ B
c) ◯ A
d) ◯ C

2.
a) F
b) T
c) T
d) T
e) T

(33)

---

1. Answers will vary

2. Answers will vary

Vocabulary

1. thrift
2. racket
3. prose
4. avoid
5. demonstrate
6. experimenting

(32)

Monarch butterfly
mini-research report

(31)

---

1. Answers will vary

2. Answers will vary

3. Answers will vary

4. Answers will vary

5. Answers will vary

6. Answers will vary

(30)

1.
a) butterflies
b) lunchbag
c) deviled crab
d) twenty dollar bill
e) batteries and a bell
f) typewriter

2.
a) 4
b) 1
c) 7
d) 6
e) 2
f) 3
g) 5

(29)

Vocabulary

1. plagiarism
2. published
3. author
4. imitate
5. rejected
6. autograph

1.
a) Mr. Badger
b) Mr. Henshaw
c) Miss Neely
d) Mrs. Badger
e) Miss Martinez
f) the judges

2.
a) ○ A   b) ○ B
c) ○ C   d) ○ B
e) ○ A   f) ○ C

---

1. Answers will vary

2. He turned red and was modest about his work. He couldn't believe that she remembered his piece.

3. Answers will vary

4. Answers will vary

5. Answers will vary

---

1. Answers will vary

2. Answers will vary

Vocabulary - Crossword

Across
2. bandanna
4. winery
5. bunk
7. sailboats
8. grove
9. grin

Down
1. tavern
3. weighscale
5. broccoli
6. rig

1.
a) 5
b) 3
c) 1
d) 7
e) 6
f) 4
g) 2

2. Answers will vary

---

1. Answers will vary

2. Answers will vary

3. Answers will vary

4. Answers will vary

5. Answers will vary

6. Answers will vary

EZ✓

Word Search Puzzle

1.
Leigh loved the book *Ways to Amuse a Dog*. It was written by Mr. Boyd Henshaw.

2.
Leigh was the first to ask ten questions so Mr. Henshaw asked him ten questions in return. His mom wouldn't get the TV fixed if he didn't answer those questions.

3.
His parents are divorced. His dad drives a rig. His mom goes to school at night to become a nurse and works at Catering by Katy.

4.
His dog is now with his dad but then he gets lost. His name is Bandit.

5.
Someone is stealing his lunch. He is lonesome because he is often left alone, he is in a new town and new school and he has no friends.

6.
He builds a burglar alarm. The man at the hardware store gave him advice but he did it alone by reading about batteries.

7.
Leigh shares all his problems with Mr. Henshaw and Pretend Mr. Henshaw (his diary). Mr. Henshaw got him started on it.

1.
a) T
b) T
c) T
d) F
e) F
f) F
g) T

2.
a) C
b) B
c) C

Bonus
A

46   45   44

Letter Writing

When writing a letter, there are certain standards, such as where to write the return address, the date, the greeting, where to write the body of the letter, the concluding remarks, the signature and the postscript. Write a proper letter, filling in the boxes with the appropriate information.